NBA CHAMPIONS

GOLDEN STATE WARRIORS

# AARON FRISCH

CREATIVE EDUCATION

Published by Creative Education
P.O. Box 227, Mankato, Minnesota 56002
Creative Education is an imprint of The Creative Company
www.thecreativecompany.us

Book and cover design by Blue Design (www.bluedes.com)
Art direction by Rita Marshall
Printed by Corporate Graphics in the United States of
America

Photographs by Corbis (Bettmann), Getty Images (Andrew
D. Bernstein/NBAE, Garrett Ellwood/NBAE, Mitchell
Funk, Jesse D. Garrabrant/NBAE, Walter Iooss Jr./Sports
Illustrated, George Long/Sports Illustrated, Hy Peskin/
Sports Illustrated, Dick Raphael/NBAE, Kent Smith/NBAE,
Rocky Widner/NBAE)

Library of Congress Cataloging-in-Publication Data

Frisch, Aaron.
Golden State Warriors / by Aaron Frisch.
p. cm. — (NBA champions)
Includes bibliographical references and index.
Summary: A basic introduction to the Golden State Warriors
professional basketball team, including its formation
in Philadelphia, Pennsylvania, in 1946, greatest players,
championships, and stars of today.
ISBN 978-1-60818-134-6
1. Golden State Warriors (Basketball team)—History—
Juvenile literature. I. Title.
GV885.52.G64F75 2011
796.323'640979461—dc22          2010050668

CPSIA: 030111 PO1448

First edition
9 8 7 6 5 4 3 2 1

*Cover: Stephen Curry*
*Page 2: Corey Maggette*
*Right: Wilt Chamberlain*
*Page 6: Jamal Crawford*

# TABLE OF CONTENTS

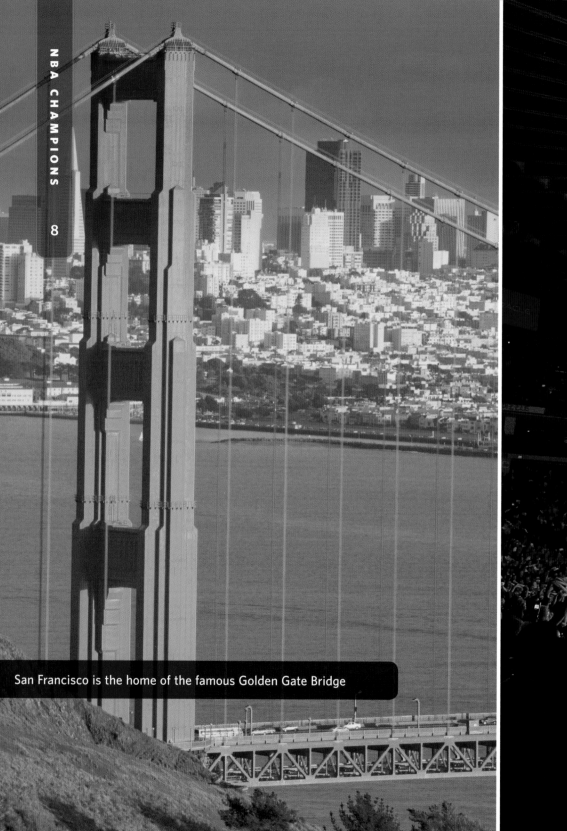

San Francisco is the home of the famous Golden Gate Bridge

California is nicknamed "The Golden State." San Francisco and Oakland are California cities that are right next to each other. Oakland has an **arena** called Oracle Arena that is the home of a basketball team called the Warriors.

Oracle Arena is the oldest arena used by an NBA team today

The Warriors are part of the National Basketball Association (NBA). All the teams in the NBA try to win the **NBA Finals** to become world champions. The Warriors play many games against teams called the Clippers, Kings, Lakers, and Suns.

Neil Johnston was the top scorer in the NBA for three straight seasons

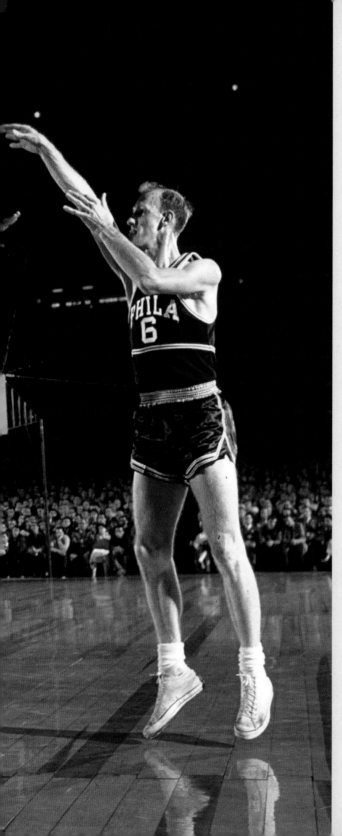

The Warriors started playing in 1946. They played in Philadelphia, Pennsylvania, then. Center Neil Johnston helped make the Warriors a tough team in the 1940s and 1950s. In 1956, Philadelphia won the NBA championship.

Rick Barry's good shooting helped the 1975 Warriors beat the Bullets

## Why Are They Called the Warriors?

The team started out in Philadelphia. In the 1920s, Philadelphia had a basketball team called the Warriors. So the new team was named that, too. California is called "The Golden State" because a lot of gold was found there in the 1800s.

In 1962, the Warriors moved to California. They got to the NBA Finals in 1964 and 1967 but lost both times. Then, in 1975, forward Rick Barry helped the Warriors beat the Washington Bullets in the NBA Finals. It was a big upset!

Tim Hardaway

## WARRIORS FACTS

- **Started playing: 1946**

- **Conference/division: Western Conference, Pacific Division**

- **Team colors: blue, orange, and yellow**

- **NBA championships:**

  **1956 — 4 games to 1 versus Fort Wayne Pistons**

  **1975 — 4 games to 0 versus Washington Bullets**

- **NBA Web site for kids: http://www.nba.com/kids/**

**T**he Warriors were not very good in the 1980s. But then they added smart coach Don Nelson and fast players like point guard Tim Hardaway. The Warriors were fun to watch when they ran **fast breaks**.

Guard Mitch Richmond was a great outside shooter

From 1995 to 2010, the

Warriors got to the **playoffs** only

one time. But fans cheered for

exciting players like Baron Davis.

He was a point guard who liked

to **drive** to the rim.

Baron Davis grew up in California and played college basketball there

TOM W RANGERS & DETRO
WED RANGERS & CHICAG
THURS MANHATTAN & ST PE
N Y U & FORDHAM
FRI BOXING TERRELL

NEW YORK
23

SAN FRANCISCO
13

SAN FRANCISCO

Warriors stars Wilt Chamberlain (above) and Nate Thurmond (opposite)

**T**he Warriors have had many stars. Wilt Chamberlain was a famous center. One time, he scored 100 points in a single game! Nate Thurmond was a center who blocked a lot of shots.

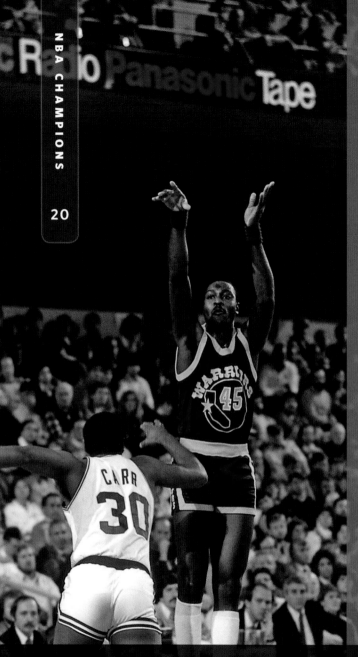

Purvis Short scored 59 points in 1 game in 1984

**S**wingman Purvis Short joined Golden State in 1978. He was one of the Warriors' best scorers for nine seasons. Forward Chris Mullin was another star. He loved to shoot three-pointers.

Chris Mullin was one of the best left-handed shooters in the NBA

Stephen Curry could score with long shots or drives to the basket

In 2009, Golden State added Stephen Curry. He was a quick guard with a great jump shot. Golden State fans hoped that he would help lead the Warriors to their third NBA championship!

# GLOSSARY

**arena** — a large building for indoor sports events; it has many seats for fans

**drive** — to dribble straight toward the basket, usually to try to get a close shot

**fast breaks** — plays in which a team runs down the basketball court and tries to score a basket quickly

**NBA Finals** — a series of games between two teams at the end of the playoffs; the first team to win four games is the champion

**swingman** — a basketball player who can play as a guard or forward

**upset** — a game in which the team that most people think will win ends up losing

# INDEX